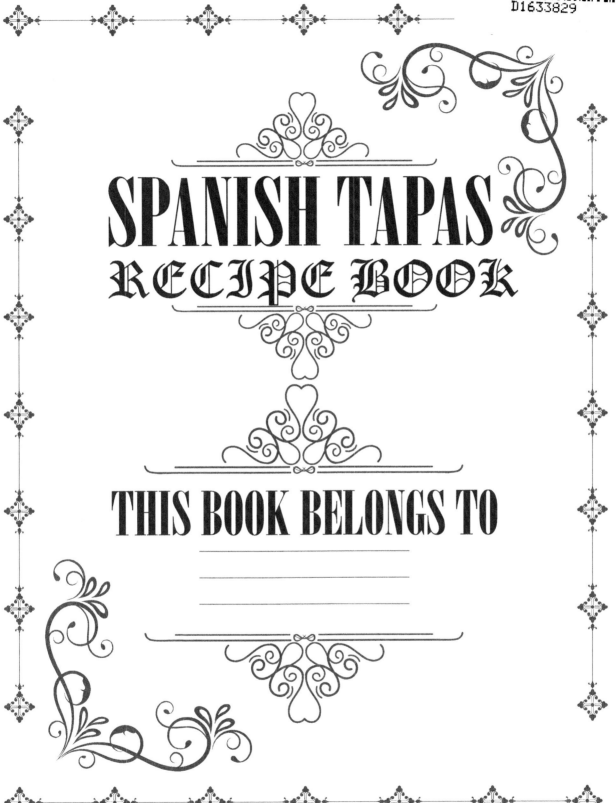

SPANISH TAPAS RECIPE BOOK

THIS BOOK BELONGS TO

TABLE OF CONTENTS

SHRIMP WITH SPICY SAFFRON SAUCE (TAPAS)FR

TUNA STUFFED PIQUILLO PEPPERS TAPAS

PEARL ONION TAPAS

PIMENTOS DE PADRON TAPAS

CHICKEN WITH LEMON AND GARLIC TAPAS

CLAMS WITH GARLIC AND ALMONDS TAPAS

SPANISH GARLIC SHRIMP

AVOCADO AND TUNA TAPAS

SPANISH STUFFED OLIVE TAPAS WITH FETA

SPANISH GARLIC TOAST

SPANISH PAN-FRIED SHRIMP WITH GARLIC

MUSHROOM CROQUETTES

SPANISH GARLIC TOAST

SPANISH STUFFED OLIVE TAPAS WITH FETA

SPANISH TORTILLA

STUFFED CHERRY PEPPERS

WARM KALE SALAD WITH ALMONDS & SERRANO HAM

PADRON PEPPERS

HAM & CHEESE CROQUETAS

ANDALUSIAN-STYLE CHICKEN

CLAMS WITH SHERRY & SERRANO HAM

HAM & PEACH NIBBLES

SAUTÉED CHORIZO WITH RED WINE

SMOKY PAPRIKA PEPPERS

FLASH-FRIED PRAWNS WITH CHILI, LEMON & PARSLEY

CRUNCHY BAKED MUSSELS

AVOCADO PUREE AND SHRIMP COCKTAIL

READY IN: 25mins

SERVES: 4-6

INGREDIENTS

- ✓ 3large avocados
- ✓ 1lb shrimp, cooked (or raw) (or raw)
- ✓ 3tablespoons extra virgin olive oil
- ✓ 1green onion, cut finely
- ✓ 1garlic clove, chopped
- ✓ salt
- ✓ 5ounces whipped cream, unsweetened
- ✓ 5tablespoons extra virgin olive oil

OPTIONAL

- ✓ shredded lettuce

DIRECTIONS

1. Season shrimp and bodies with salt and pepper and cook lightly in oil; set aside.
2. Using a hand blender, peel avocados, remove pits, and crush/mush with green onion, garlic, olive oil, and cream to produce a silky smooth purée—season with salt and pepper to taste.

3. Line the bottom of a cocktail dish with shredded lettuce (optional), then alternate layers of shrimp and avocado purée.

4. Refrigerate until ready to serve.

ASPARAGUS W/ORANGE AND LEMON SAUCE

READY IN: 20mins

SERVES: 4

INGREDIENTS

✓ 1 (15 oz) white asparagus can (or green)

SAUCE

✓ Two hard-boiled egg yolks

✓ One egg yolk

✓ 1tsp lemon juice

✓ 1 tsp orange juice

✓ 1 tsp salt and pepper

✓ 1/2c olive oil

✓ One white egg

✓ 1orange, cut

✓ One lemon slices

DIRECTIONS

1. In a sieve, drain the asparagus.

2. Chop the hard-boiled egg yolks into small pieces and combine them with the raw egg yolk.

3. Salt and pepper and add the orange and lemon juices.

4. Add the olive oil gradually, pounding as though making mayonnaise.

5. Season to taste.

6. Add the egg whites to the sauce after beating until stiff.

7. Arrange the well-drained asparagus on a serving dish, drizzle with sauce, and garnish with orange and lemon slices.

SPANISH KEBABS/TAPAS

READY IN: 20mins

YIELD: 8 tapas

INGREDIENTS

- ✓ 2 tbsp chopped onions
- ✓ Four garlic, chopped
- ✓ 1 tsp sweet smoked paprika
- ✓ 1/4 tsp cayenne or 1/2tsp smoked paprika
- ✓ salt (kosher or sea)
- ✓ 1 t dried oregano
- ✓ 1 tsp black pepper
- ✓ 2 tsp dried thyme
- ✓ 1 tsp cumin
- ✓ 1/8 teaspoon cinnamon
- ✓ One crushed bay leaf
- ✓ 2 tbsp white wine vinegar (good quality)
- ✓ 2 tsp dry white wine (optional)
- ✓ Three plus extra for brushing the kebabs
- ✓ 1 1/2 chicken breasts or prawns

DIRECTIONS

1. In a bit of food processor, process the onion, garlic, sweet and spicy paprikas, two teaspoons salt, oregano, peppercorns, thyme, cumin, cinnamon, bay leaf, vinegar, wine (if used), and olive oil to a paste.

2. Place the pork in a basin and season with salt. Scrape the marinade into the bowl with the meat and toss to coat evenly with the marinade.

3. Wrap the bowl in plastic and chill the pork for 4-6 hours, tossing occasionally. Let the meat warm up before grilling.

4. Preheat the grill to medium-high or preheat a big ridged grill pan over medium heat to medium-high.

5. Thread the meat onto the skewers and spray with a bit of olive oil when ready to cook.

6. Cook the beef, coating with olive oil and flipping once, for 5-7 minutes, or until it is just cooked through. (If you're preparing lamb and prefer it medium-rare, reduce the cooking time slightly.) Serve the kebabs immediately.

GRILLED GOAT'S CHEESE ON A BED OF LETTUCE

READY IN: 20mins

SERVES: 4-6

INGREDIENTS

- ✓ 11 oz goat cheese
- ✓ 1 tsp oil
- ✓ 4 cups Baby Spinach

VINAIGRETTE

- ✓ 1/2 virgin olive oil
- ✓ 3 tbsp sherry vinegar wine
- ✓ 1 tsp honey

- ✓ Seasoning

DIRECTIONS

1. Preheat oven to grill mode.
2. Vinaigrette:
3. Salt, pepper, and honey in a small bowl. Add the virgin olive oil and whisk until an emulsion forms.
4. Slice the cheese 3/4 inch thick and cook until brown in the oven.
5. Arrange baby greens on plates, drizzle with vinaigrette, and top with cheese.

Spanish Tortilla Recipe

Prep Time: 1 hour

Cook Time: 15 minutes

Total Time: 1 hour 15 minutes

Servings: 8 slices

INGREDIENTS

- ✓ 2 lb Yukon Golds (1kg)
- ✓ SALT TO TASTE
- ✓ Eight big free-range eggs
- ✓ One big onion
- ✓ EVOO to saute the potatoes and cook the tortilla. You can use a neutral oil for frying (although good olive oil makes a difference!).

Instructions

1. Rinse the potatoes in cool water.

2. Thinly slice the potatoes; I prefer around 1/2 centimeter thick (some prefer thicker). I accomplish this quickly and effortlessly with a mandolin.

3. Pat the potato slices dry and combine them in a large mixing dish with the salt.

4. Heat a 1/2 inch of excellent quality extra virgin olive oil in a big frying pan over medium-low heat.

5. Add the potatoes and enough oil to coat them completely.

6. Cook the potatoes on low heat for 20 minutes (they may break apart, that is okay).

7. While the potatoes simmer, beat the eggs with a bit of salt in a large mixing bowl.

8. Slice the onion as thinly as possible (julienne style) and cook for approximately 10-20 minutes over low heat in a separate heavy pan (I prefer stainless steel) until they begin to caramelize (stir often).

9. Drain any extra oil from the caramelized onions and add to the egg mixture.

10. After 20 minutes of cooking, remove the potatoes with a slotted spoon to a strainer and leave to cool while any extra oil drips away.

11. Add the potatoes after a few minutes.

12. Allow approximately 20 minutes for the egg mixture to rest.

13. In the same pan, to fry the potatoes, drain all the oil (it may be reused!) and add the egg mixture over medium-low heat.

14. Cook the tortilla for approximately 6-8 minutes per side over medium-low heat. Assure that the heat is turned down low enough; else,

the tortilla will cook too rapidly and become rubbery. You can run a rubber spatula down the tortilla's edges to ensure it does not cling.

15. When the tortilla's bottom is cooked and you're ready to turn it, swiftly place a large plate over the pan and flip! Some egg will almost certainly escape– it'll be a mess– but that's fine!

16. Lastly, turn the pan out onto a serving tray and set it aside to cool somewhat before diving in.

Spanish Tomato Bread

Prep Time: 15 minutes

Total Time: 15 minutes

Servings: 10 servings

Ingredients

- ✓ Four tomatoes ripe and juicy
- ✓ EVOO to taste
- ✓ One garlic clove halved
- ✓ SALT TO TASTE
- ✓ One rustic loaf of unleavened bread (works best for avoiding sogginess and maintaining crunchiness)
- ✓ Six thin slices of Spanish Serrano or Iberian ham are optional but preferred

Instructions

1. Cut the bread into medium-thick toast pieces. Arrange the bread pieces on a baking pan and toast for approximately five to ten minutes at 250°F (120°C), rotating halfway through.

2. Thoroughly clean and dry the tomatoes. They should be cut in half and grated with a box grater, stems, and skins removed.

3. Once the tomatoes are grated, set aside in a small bowl and season with a touch of salt and around one tablespoon olive oil. Adjust to taste as necessary.

4. Halve the garlic clove and smear the raw garlic all over the toasted bread. Then spoon the tomato mixture gently onto the garlic toast pieces, drizzle with extra virgin olive oil, and sprinkle with sea salt.

5. Optionally, garnish with a slice of Serrano or Iberian jamón for added flavor and a heartier toast. Enjoy!

Notes

1. Use only the most delicate stuff here — you will taste it!

2. Toppings: You can get creative with your pan con tomate to make it more feast. Several classic Spanish combinations include the following:

3. Jamón, as well as other cured meats such as lomo or fuet

4. Anchovies, both cured in salt and marinated (boquerones en vinagre). When one of each is used, it is referred to as a "matrimonio" (marriage).

5. Cheese: A simple slice of cheese might serve as the ideal complement.

Traditional Spanish Ham Croquettes

Prep Time: 30 minutes

Cook Time: 15 minutes

Total Time: 45 minutes

Servings: 24 croquettes

Ingredients

✓ 1 tbsp unsalted (60 g)

- ✓ 1/4 CUP OIL (60 ml)
- ✓ 1 cup flour (120 g)
- ✓ One medium onion, diced
- ✓ 1/4 gallon whole milk (1 liter)
- ✓ 1 tsp nutmeg
- ✓ 1/2 pound serrano jamón diced (225 g)
- ✓ breading flour
- ✓ Two eggs beaten
- ✓ bread crumbs (try Panko for super crispy croquettes!)

Instructions

1. Preheat the oil and butter in a big pot over medium heat.
2. Add the diced onion and cook for a few minutes, or until it begins to brown slightly.
3. Season with a touch of salt and nutmeg. If necessary, add a little salt, as the Serrano ham is pretty salty.
4. Add the diced ham and sauté for an additional 30 seconds.
5. Stir in the flour continually until it turns a light brown hue. You must continue stirring at all times, or the flour will burn!
6. Add milk when the flour turns color in tiny amounts, constantly stirring until the total amount is incorporated. It should take approximately 15-20 minutes to combine everything.
7. Remove from the fire and chill the dough to room temperature.
8. Brush the sides of a big mixing bowl with butter and set the croquette dough inside, directly covered with plastic wrap. Refrigerate for four hours or overnight.

9. Shape the ham croquettes into little logs (or use a pastry sleeve if you have one.)

10. Next, pass the croquettes through the three-step breading procedure while heating a pan of olive oil on the stove. Cover them first with flour, then with egg, and finally with breadcrumbs.

11. Heat the oil for the ham croquettes. around five minutes (turning halfway through to ensure even browning) and then set aside to cool for a few minutes before serving!

Notes

1. The technique to make creamy croquettes is to add the milk gently and constantly mix.

2. Prosciutto or Iberian ham may be substituted for the jamón Serrano — or any other high-quality cured ham.

3. The breaded prepared croquette logs can quickly be frozen. They'll last three months in the freezer.

4. Refrigerate leftovers for 3 days. Reheat in a hot oven (350°F/170°C) for 10 minutes.

Spanish Broken Eggs with Ham, Chorizo, & Peppers

Prep Time: 10 minutes

Cook Time: 30 minutes

Total Time: 40 minutes

Servings: 4 servings

Ingredients

✓ 4 POTATOES 1 per person

✓ 4 Eggs

- ✓ One big onion
- ✓ 1/2 cup sliced green peppers
- ✓ Thin Iberian or Serrano ham or prosciutto slices
- ✓ One cured Spanish chorizo link
- ✓ Five minced garlic cloves
- ✓ 1 tsp parsley
- ✓ Olive oil
- ✓ SALT & PEPPER

Instructions

1. Olive oil the pan's bottom and heat over medium heat. Add the onions.

2. Thinly slice the potatoes and add to the pan.

3. Add the garlic, parsley, and peppers and reduce to low heat.

4. Cover and stir every ten minutes gently.

5. Cook for approximately 30 minutes (until all potatoes are tender and starting to brown)

6. Scatter the four eggs evenly over the potatoes and reduce the heat to a shallow setting. Cook the eggs, covered, just until the whites have set. Then, separate the yolks and take the pan off the heat!

7. Meanwhile, dice the chorizo into rounds (or remove the casing and crumble), then brown in a separate pan over medium heat.

Season with salt and pepper to taste.

9. Top the potatoes and eggs with thin slices of ham (no need to cook the ham if using decent ham) and fried chorizo.

Traditional Spanish Pisto Recipe

Prep Time: 10 minutes

Cook Time: 25 minutes

Total Time: 35 minutes

Servings: 4 servings

Ingredients

- ✓ Three small sliced zucchini
- ✓ Two diced medium red bell peppers
- ✓ Two chopped medium green bell peppers
- ✓ Four medium diced onions
- ✓ Three tiny purple eggplants, sliced
- ✓ 2 lbs ripe tomatoes Better tomatoes, better piste! diced
- ✓ Five garlic cloves diced
- ✓ Pinch of thyme rosemary and/or oregano
- ✓ 1 tsp cumin
- ✓ 1 tsp refined sugar (honey or brown sugar for a natural approach)
- ✓ Salt and pepper to taste
- ✓ Optional dried cayenne peppers (not typical)
- ✓ olive oil
- ✓ Fried eggs
- ✓ Any cured raw sheep's milk cheese, such as Manchego

Instructions

1. Peel and dice the veggies according to the directions on the package, then place the eggplant on paper towels before seasoning with kosher salt. Allow them to sit for 10 minutes.

2. Heat two separate frying pans over medium heat, each with a dab of olive oil.

3. In one of the pots, add the diced onions and a touch of salt. Sauté until they turn transparent, then cover the pan and let them poach (you do not want them to be brown). Once thoroughly cooked, transfer to a large bowl.

4. Meanwhile, in the other pan, add the peppers and sauté over medium-high heat until they brown. Reduce to medium heat and cover for approximately 10 minutes. Once done, set aside with the onions.

5. Using a mesh strainer, rinse the eggplant to remove excess salt.

6. Cook the zucchini and eggplant in the same manner as the peppers (in separate pans). You want to begin cooking them on medium-high heat, and once they start to brown, reduce to low heat and cover until cooked (occasionally turning to prevent them from sticking). Then reserve with the remaining vegetables, tossing to incorporate all flavors.

7. Combine all of the seasonings in the dish of vegetables.

8. Next, if necessary, add a bit of extra oil to one of the pans and if using dried cayenne peppers, chopped garlic. Sauté over medium heat until the onions begin to brown. Then, in the same pan, add the peeled and diced tomato. Cook, constantly stirring, for around 20 minutes over medium-low heat until you have tomato sauce. Add the sugar and season with salt to taste.

9. In a large frying pan, combine the cooked vegetables and tomato sauce.

10. Combine all ingredients and cook for 10 minutes over medium heat. Enjoy with salt and spices to taste!

1. Optional Additions: The most popular pisto meals in Spain are piste con huevos (pesto topped with a fried egg) and pisto Manchego (pesto with sliced Manchego cheese on top). Both are excellent ways to serve your pisto as a meal or a side dish for fish or meat.

Spanish Padron Peppers Recipe

Prep Time: 5 minutes

Cook Time: 5 minutes

Total Time: 10 minutes

Servings: 4 servings

Ingredients

- ✓ 300 g Padron peppers (approximately 2 cups)
- ✓ 50 ml extra virgin olive oil
- ✓ Flaky salt

Instructions

1. Rinse and pat the peppers dry.
2. Heat the olive oil in a saucepan over high heat until it is boiling (but not yet smoking).
3. Cook, occasionally stirring, until the skin of the peppers begins to blister and soften. Allow them to soften completely without allowing them to burn.
4. Transfer the peppers to a platter.
5. Drizzle liberally with sea salt and serve!

Notes

1. Shishito peppers are an excellent replacement for Padron peppers.

2. For the most delicate flavor, use sea salt. I particularly enjoy using flakes of sea salt, such as Maldon salt.

3. When frying, use high-quality olive oil; these peppers are designed to be pretty fatty, so the higher the quality of the olive oil, the better they'll taste!

4. Keep an eye out for flying oil splatters and allow the peppers to cool for a few minutes before eating!

Spinach and Chickpeas

Prep Time: 10 minutes

Cook Time: 20 minutes

Total Time: 30 minutes

Servings: 4 servings

<u>Ingredients</u>

✓ One jar garbanzo beans (around 500g or 18 ounces) you could also soak and cook dry garbanzos for a more flavorful outcome, but i prefer the convenience of good quality canned beans.

✓ 10 oz. Cleaned spinach (one large bag or 300 g/10 oz.)

✓ Two thick day-old sourdough slices, sliced into cubes

✓ 15 blanched unsalted marcona

✓ 1/4 cups tomato sauce (60ml)

✓ Three sliced garlic cloves

✓ Oil

✓ If sherry vinegar is unavailable, use red wine vinegar instead.

✓ 1 tsp cumin

✓ 1 tsp ground cayenne pepper

- ✓ 1 tsp salt (more to taste)
- ✓ Pepper to taste
- ✓ 1 tsp smoked paprika i use dulce pimentón, but you could use picante.

Instructions

1. Coat a big saucepan with extra virgin olive oil (about 2 tbsp) and place over medium-high heat.

2. Add the spinach to the oil just before it becomes too hot (in batches if necessary)

3. Sauté the spinach until barely wilted and removed to drain colander.

4. Re-oil the pan and add the bread pieces and raw almonds. Fry until the bread and almonds are toasted and crispy on both sides.

5. Add the chopped garlic, cumin, cayenne pepper, and black pepper and sauté for a few minutes, or until the garlic is fragrant and beginning to brown.

6. In a blender/food processor, combine the ingredients and add the sherry vinegar.

7. Combine the ingredients until a thick paste form (add a few tablespoons of water if necessary to make blending more accessible, but avoid making it mushy).

8. Transfer the paste back to the pot and combine with the garbanzo beans and tomato sauce.

9. Gently stir until the chickpeas are completely coated with the sauce, and add a splash of water if necessary.

10. Stir in the spinach gently until uniformly distributed and heated. Season with salt and pepper to taste.

12. Drizzle a swirl of extra virgin olive oil on top of each dish after plating, followed by a sprinkle of smoky Spanish paprika.

Enjoy!

Fried Eggplant with Honey

Prep Time: 1 hour

Cook Time: 15 minutes

Total Time: 1 hour 15 minutes

Servings: 4 servings

Ingredients

- ✓ 2–3 tiny eggplants
- ✓ Covered in milk
- ✓ 1 Salt (TBS)
- ✓ 2 tsp pepper
- ✓ Flour
- ✓ Olive oil for frying
- ✓ Drizzle with honey or molasses

Instructions

1. Depending on your liking, cut the eggplant into round slices or matchsticks.

2. Cover the eggplant with milk and season with a bit of salt in a big basin. Allow about an hour for the eggplant to soak (to draw out any bitterness).

3. Drain the eggplant and cover each slice in flour, seasoning with salt and pepper to taste.

4. Fry the pieces in a large, heavy skillet with plenty of olive oil. (Ensure the oil is very heated before adding the slices and fry in batches to prevent the pan from becoming overcrowded!)

5. Drain the eggplant on paper towels. Add a pinch of salt to taste. Before serving, drizzle with honey or molasses.

Mediterranean Roast Vegetables

Prep Time: 10 minutes

Cook Time: 30 minutes

Servings: 6 people

Ingredients

- ✓ Baby potatoes, 8 oz.
- ✓ 8 ounces Roma tomatoes (any little sweet tomato would do)
- ✓ Two zucchinis, diced
- ✓ Two red bell peppers, diced
- ✓ Two medium eggplants, diced
- ✓ One garlic clove, peeled
- ✓ 1/3 cup Oil
- ✓ 1 tbsp thyme (sub dried if necessary)
- ✓ 1 tbsp oregano (sub dried if necessary)
- ✓ salt and pepper

Instructions

1. Preheat oven to 425°F (220 degrees Celsius) and gently oil a large roasting pan or ceramic baking dish.

2. Mix all the vegetables and garlic in a big basin. Drizzle with olive oil and pepper.Toss in salt and pepper to taste. Assemble everything in a single layer of oil for the ideal roast and caramelization.

3. Remove the potatoes from the oven and set them in the roasting pan. After ten minutes, take the pan from the oven and stir in the remaining vegetables and garlic. 20-25 minutes longer, or until all vegetables are soft.(A few burned black parts are acceptable!).

4. Immediately remove from oven and serve. Additionally, you may grate fresh parmesan or Manchego cheese over the top for added taste!

Notes

1. Spread your vegetables out on a big baking sheet to achieve the best results. I prefer baking directly on the sheet, but parchment paper can be used if necessary.

2. Vegetables should never be covered! This makes them steam and mushy.

3. Refrain from moving them around while cooking. We want them to adhere and caramelize somewhat.

4. Before serving, taste and adjust the seasoning with additional sea salt.

5. Before serving, sprinkle a pinch of pimentón de la Vera (smoked Spanish paprika) on top.

Goat Cheese and Caramelized Onion Pintxo

Prep Time: 20 minutes

Cook Time: 40 minutes

Total Time: 1 hour

Servings: 12 servings

Ingredients

- ✓ 1 tbsp olive oil
- ✓ One large onion, sliced
- ✓ 1 tsp salt
- ✓ 1/2 cup brown sugar
- ✓ 1/2 tsp balsamic sherry vinegar
- ✓ 12 French baguettes 1" thick
- ✓ One chevre goat cheese packet
- ✓ Two rosemary sprigs
- ✓ Optional toothpicks/skewers

Instructions

1. Heat the olive oil in a large skillet over medium-high heat. Once heated through, add in the onions and simmer for 10 minutes, stirring constantly.

2. Reduce to medium-low heat and whisk in the salt, sugar, and vinegar. Cook, stirring every 4-5 minutes, for approximately 30 minutes, or until the onions are a deep, dark brown and taste sweet and tender. If you're going to leave the onions in the pan to caramelize while doing anything else, keep a splash of water in the pan to prevent them from burning. Allow at least 10 minutes for cooling.

3. heat oven to 325°F. Bake the baguette slices for 6-8 minutes, or until gently toasted.

4. To assemble the pintxos, spread a heaping teaspoon of onion on each slice of bread and top with a heaping teaspoon or large piece (depending on the variety) of goat cheese. Garnish with a few rosemary leaves at room temperature.

Marinated Carrots

Prep Time: 25 minutes

Cook Time: 4 hours 30 minutes

Total Time: 4 hours 55 minutes

Servings: 4 servings

Ingredients

- ✓ 6-7 big carrots
- ✓ 2-4 cloves garlic I suggest you start with less garlic.
- ✓ 1 T dried oregano
- ✓ 4 t cumin
- ✓ 1 t smoked Spanish paprika
- ✓ 1/3 c apple cider vinegar (or mild vinegar)
- ✓ SALT TO TASTE
- ✓ olive oil

Instructions

1. Bring a half-gallon of water to a boil in a saucepan with a teaspoon of salt.
2. After washing and peeling the carrots, add them to the boiling water.
3. Bring the carrots to a boil and simmer until just tender—do not overcook! Then drain and chill in cold water.
4. Mash the garlic and spices until a paste forms.
5. Once the carrots have cooled, cut them into large round slices and place them in your serving bowl.

6. Stir in the garlic paste and add equal parts vinegar and water until the carrots are completely covered with liquid.

7. Cover the carrots and refrigerate for a minimum of 4 hours.

8. Using a slotted spoon, scoop the out of the liquid and serve with a drizzle of high-quality olive oil and a sprinkling of salt.

Patatas Bravas Recipe

Prep Time: 5 minutes

Cook Time: 15 minutes

Total Time: 20 minutes

Servings: 4 servings

Ingredients

- ✓ One medium potato
- ✓ 1-2 cups olive oil for frying
- ✓ salt
- ✓ 1/2 cup homemade bravas sauce

Instructions

1. Peel the potatoes, thoroughly rinse them, and dry them with a paper towel.

2. Chop the potatoes into small bite-size pieces.

3. Heat the olive oil in a large skillet over medium heat.

4. Reduce heat and add potatoes to the lowest setting for a few minutes to allow them to pre-cook.

5. Removing the potatoes from the oven and place them in the refrigerator to cool for a few minutes longer.

6. Increase the heat to high and reintroduce the potatoes to the pan.

7. Fry till golden and crusty.

8. Drain the potatoes on a paper towel-lined platter and season with salt to taste.

9. Drizzle the bravas sauce over the potatoes to serve.

10. Dig in with your hands—no forks required!

Patatas Alioli

Prep Time: 10 minutes

Cook Time: 30 minutes

Total Time: 40 minutes

Servings: 4 servings

__Ingredients__

- ✓ Four medium potatoes, unpeeled
- ✓ Three cloves garlic
- ✓ 1/2 tsp salt
- ✓ One egg yolk
- ✓ 3/4 cup extra virgin olive
- ✓ 1 tsp lemon juice
- ✓ 1 tbsp chopped parsley

Instructions

1. Thoroughly wash the potatoes and then lay them in a saucepan with enough cold water to cover them.

2. Bring water to a boil. 15 minutes covered or until potatoes are done. Allow cooling slightly before peeling (roughly 15 minutes).

3. Prepare the sauce while the potatoes cool. Peel and mince the garlic, then pound it using a mortar and pestle into a paste.

4. In the hand/stick blender container, combine the garlic paste and egg yolk. To blend, softly pulse.

5. Add the olive oil gradually to the mixture, mixing gently to integrate it as you pour. As the oil emulsifies, the mixture should thicken progressively. Once the oil is thoroughly blended, add the lemon juice and blend until smooth.

6. Once cooled and peeled, slice the potatoes into 1-inch cubes. Coat with aioli and sprinkle with parsley.

Spanish Potato Salad

Prep Time: 10 minutes

Cook Time: 1 hour 30 minutes

Total Time: 1 hour 40 minutes

Servings: 4 servings

Ingredients

- ✓ 3 lb medium fresh potatoes
- ✓ Two tiny white onions
- ✓ water
- ✓ Parsley, diced
- ✓ olive oil, especially a spicy Andalusian picual
- ✓ 4 tbsp Sherry vinegar
- ✓ saline
- ✓ Two cooked eggs
- ✓ Two cans of premium Spanish tuna

Instructions

1. Thoroughly wash the potatoes, place them in a large saucepan, and fill them with water.

2. Cook over high heat and immediately add a tablespoon of sea salt when the water begins to boil. 3. Allow the potatoes to cook until just soft (when a toothpick/fork can be twisted through them). This process should take approximately 25 minutes.

3. Dice the onion and parsley while the potatoes are cooking.

4. Turn off the heat and continue cooking the potatoes in the heated water for another 30 minutes.

5. Spoon out the potatoes and let them cool for 20 minutes in a strainer.

6. Using your hands or a knife, scrape away the skin.

7. Place the potatoes in a glass basin.

8. Combine the onion, parsley, and 1/2 teaspoon sea salt.

9. Finally, add the vinegar and olive oil.

10. Season to taste with salt and arrange the tuna can (drained) on top, along with the sliced hard-boiled egg.

11. Enjoy!

Poor Man's Potatoes "Papas a lo Pobre."

Prep Time: 5 minutes

Cook Time: 15 minutes

Total Time: 20 minutes

Servings: 4 -6 people

Ingredients

✓ 4-6 medium potatoes

- ✓ Two onions
- ✓ Two green peppers
- ✓ olive oil
- ✓ 3 garlic cloves
- ✓ salt
- ✓ Pepper

Instructions

1. Wash, peel, and finely slice your potatoes.
2. Cut the onions, green peppers, and garlic into small pieces.
3. In a large skillet, heat a generous amount of olive oil over low heat and sauté the potatoes until they begin to soften. Continue to move the potatoes carefully to prevent them from frying.
4. Add the green peppers, onions, and garlic when the potatoes soften.
5. Cook, occasionally stirring, until the potatoes, peppers, and onions are very tender.
6. Pour off any extra olive oil.
7. Add salt and pepper to taste.
8. Serve as a side dish and enjoy!

Chorizo Cooked in Cider

Prep Time: 5 minutes

Cook Time: 15 minutes

Total Time: 20 minutes

Servings: 6 servings

Ingredients

- ✓ 500 g fresh or semi-cured chorizo
- ✓ 1 tbsp extra virgin olive oil
- ✓ 1.5 cups apple cider
- ✓ Two bay leaf
- ✓ 2 tbsp parsley, chopped

Instructions

1. Cut the chorizo into 2-centimeter (just under 1-inch) pieces and set aside.
2. Pre-heat the olive oil.
3. Cook the chorizo in the pan, occasionally stirring, until the pieces begin to brown (roughly 5 minutes).
4. Toss the chorizo in the cider and bay leaves to coat. Simmer for 5-8 minutes, or until the cider becomes syrupy and the chorizo leaves streaks of red oil on top.
5. Garnish with parsley if desired.

Fried Pork Rolls

Prep Time: 10 minutes

Cook Time: 20 minutes

Total Time: 30 minutes

Servings: 4 servings

Ingredients

- ✓ Four pork fillets, each around 150g
- ✓ Two minced garlic cloves
- ✓ One lemon juice

- ✓ 1.5 tsp dried parsley
- ✓ 1 tsp salt
- ✓ 1/4 pounds/120g Jamon serrano
- ✓ 1/4 pound / 120g Gruyere cheese chopped into 1/2-inch broad sticks
- ✓ Flour
- ✓ Two beaten eggs
- ✓ 120 g / 1/4 lb breadcrumbs
- ✓ frying olive oil

Instructions

1. Place the pork fillets between two sheets of plastic wrap and flatten with a meat mallet to a maximum thickness of 1/4-inch.

2. Remove the plastic wrap from the pork and set it in a small bowl. Marinate the garlic, lemon juice, parsley, and salt in the refrigerator for 1-2 hours.

3. Take out the meat and flatten it. Completely cover the pork fillets with a thin layer of Jamon serrano, and then arrange the sticks of cheese end-to-end down one of the long edges.

4. Gently roll the pork and ham into a log around the cheese sticks, forming the outer layer of the record with the pork. Each log should be moved in flour, beaten egg, and last in breadcrumbs.

5. Meanwhile, heat a big heavy skillet over medium-high heat and fill halfway with olive oil.

6. Once the oil is hot, cook the flamenquines in batches, opening side down in the pan. Each side should be roasted until browned to ensure the meat is cooked through and the cheese is gooey. Remove the flamenquines from the

pan and drain any leftover oil on a paper towel. Serve immediately with a garden salad and/or french fries.

Spanish Bull Tail Stew

Prep Time: 15 minutes

Cook Time: 3 hours 10 minutes

Total Time: 3 hours 25 minutes

Servings: 4 servings

Ingredients

- ✓ 4-6 lbs Rabo de toro (oxtail, cow tail, etc.)
- ✓ Three sliced carrots
- ✓ Two sweet onion diced
- ✓ One diced red bell
- ✓ One leek, diced
- ✓ 2-3 tomatoes sliced
- ✓ Four minced garlic cloves
- ✓ 2 cups beef stock
- ✓ 3 c red wine a good table wine like a Spanish rioja or tempranillo
- ✓ Two bay leaves
- ✓ Four cloves
- ✓ 1 tsp ground ginger
- ✓ Salt
- ✓ Pepper
- ✓ Meat in flour
- ✓ Olive oil

Instructions

2. Salt and pepper the bull tail.

3. Heat a splash of olive oil in a large, heavy pan (cast iron works well) over medium-high heat (not yet smoking).

4. Lightly coat the Rabo de toro with flour (shake off excess) and sear each piece in the hot oil for about 30 seconds per side, or until beautifully browned.

5. Discard the bull tail and set the pieces aside to dry.

6. Saute the leek, onion, garlic, red pepper, and tomato in the pan's oil for approximately 10 minutes.

7. Cook for 1 minute before adding the carrots, bay leaves, ginger, and cloves.

8. Return the bull tail to the pan and add the wine and stock.

9. Bring to a moderate simmer, covered.

10. After 3 hours, check to see if the Rabo de toro is falling away from the bone. It may take an additional hour if the meat is extremely tough.

11. If the beef is sufficiently cooked, remove it and purée the sauce with a hand blender (not necessary but nice).

12. Accompany with homemade french fries or mashed potatoes for a truly authentic Spanish supper!

Notes

1. Flour: Dusting the oxtail with flour assists in the formation of a thick and delectable sauce, but it can be omitted without affecting the flavor.

2. Wine: Use a decent red wine — nothing fancy, but something drinkable. It imparts a great deal of flavor to the stew! Antonia occasionally substitutes sherry or brandy for some of the red wine.

3. Spices: While ginger is not a traditional component, I adore it! You may omit if you choose. Additionally, if you prefer a more spiced flavor, add additional cloves.

4. Substitutions for Osso Bucco, beef shanks, beef short ribs on the bone, veal neck, and veal shank: Oxtail can easily be substituted for Osso Bucco, beef shanks, beef short ribs on the bone, veal neck, and veal shank.

5. Additions: After puréeing the sauce, Antonia occasionally adds a little something extra to this dish. Mushrooms and pearl onions are two options. Both are delectable.

6. Time is your ally; it may take more than three hours. When finished, it should be soft and fall off the bone. If in doubt, continue!

7. You can use a pressure cooker; simply adjust the time accordingly.

Braised Iberian Pork Cheek with Port Wine and Honey

Prep Time: 30 minutes

Cook Time: 3 hours

Total Time: 3 hours 30 minutes

Servings: 4 servings

Ingredients

- ✓ 12 Iberian pork cheeks (1 kg/2 pound)
- ✓ One onion
- ✓ Six shallots

- ✓ One green apple
- ✓ Two carrots
- ✓ One red pepper
- ✓ Two garlic cloves
- ✓ 2 cups port wine dessert wine
- ✓ 24 fingerlings or 4-5 regular potatoes
- ✓ One bay leaf
- ✓ 2 tsp honey
- ✓ 1/2 tsp thyme
- ✓ 1/2 tsp fresh parsley
- ✓ One teaspoon salt and pepper
- ✓ 2 tbsp flour
- ✓ 1/3 cup Oil
- ✓ 3 c beef stock

Instructions

1. In a mortar and pestle, pound the garlic and add the thyme, honey, parsley, and a tablespoon of water. Continue mashing until smooth paste forms.
2. Using paper towels, pat the pork cheeks completely dry, then top with the pasta and season with kosher salt and pepper. Allow at least an hour for marinating before cooking.
3. After about an hour, quickly dredge the pig cheeks in flour (they should not be coated entirely; a trace of flour should remain).
4. Heat olive oil in a big pan

5. Sear the pork cheeks (about 30 seconds on each of its three or four sides) until browned on all sides.

6. Once each cheek has been seared, take it from the pan and set it aside.

7. Finely dice the onion and red pepper.

8. Peel and chop the shallots in half.

9. Thinly slice the carrots into circular slices.

10. Pour the oil used to sear the meat into a large, heavy saucepan. If required, add a bit extra oil to completely cover the bottom, around 1 centimeter.

11. Sauté the onions, peppers, shallots, and carrots for 15 minutes over low heat.

12. Add the pork cheek and 2 cups port wine to the veggies when they are browned (any port will do, although there are various varieties of port wine, and each will leave you with a slightly different dish)

13. Add the bay leaf and cook, occasionally stirring, until everything has reduced by half, about 15 minutes. Stir constantly while it thickens, or it will stick.

14. Remove the peel from the potatoes (if using large potatoes, cut them into bite-size chunks).

15. Peel and dice the apple into medium dice.

16. Pour in the beef stock and simmer over low heat for approximately 1.5 hours, or until the carrilladas are thoroughly soft. Add the potatoes and apple to the saucepan for twenty minutes before turning off the heat.

17. When the vegetables are fork-tender, remove them from the fire and serve.

Prep Time: 5 minutes

Cook Time: 15 minutes

Total Time: 20 minutes

Servings: 12 servings

Ingredients

- ✓ Six pieces thinly sliced bacon (or serrano ham or prosciutto)
- ✓ 12 big dates
- ✓ 3 oz goat cheese
- ✓ 12 toothpicks
- ✓ 12 Marcona almonds (optional)

Instructions

1. 350°F oven (175 degrees Celsius).

2. To prepare the dates, cut lengthwise into each one from the edge to the pit with a sharp knife. Remove the hole carefully and replace it with a tiny bit of goat cheese (and the almond if used). Seal the dates by pressing the edges together.

3. Halve the bacon strips and wrap one piece of bacon around each date. With a toothpick, secure the bacon, dates, and cheese together, ensuring that the cheese is secured inside.

4. Evenly distribute the dates in a baking dish with raised lips, leaving space between each one. Bake for approximately 15 minutes, flipping halfway through, or until the bacon is crispy and brown.

Prep Time: 10 minutes

Cook Time: 10 minutes

Total Time: 20 minutes

Servings: 6 servings

Ingredients

- ✓ 18 Asparagus sprigs 2-3 per person, cut ends
- ✓ olive Oil
- ✓ 1/3 pound (200g) cured ham thinly sliced (Iberian, Serrano, or Prosciutto)
- ✓ black pepper
- ✓ Manchego grated cheese

Instructions

1. Aluminum foil a baking sheet and preheat the oven to 425 degrees Fahrenheit.
2. Coat the asparagus spears with extra virgin olive oil and freshly ground black pepper in a large bowl or baking dish (remember that the cured ham and Manchego cheese are both salty, so skip adding extra salt here)
3. Wrap cured ham around each asparagus spear. If your ham slices are exceptionally huge, you may just need half for each spear. To completely wrap the asparagus, roll on the diagonal.
4. Arrange each wrapped spear on the baking sheet, ensuring they do not touch (otherwise, they will steam rather than crisp).
5. Drizzle with a drizzle of olive oil
6. 5 minutes in the oven, center.

7. Remove from oven and flip each ham-wrapped asparagus spear over to crisp up both sides. Return to the oven and sprinkle manchego cheese on top.

8. Bake for a further five minutes and, if the top has not yet browned, increase the heat to broil just until golden.

9. Turn off the heat.

10.   Serve immediately or set aside and quickly reheat before serving.

Spanish Garlic Shrimp

Prep Time: 10 minutes

Cook Time: 10 minutes

Total Time: 20 minutes

Ingredients

- ✓ 1 pound (0.5 kg) tiny raw shrimp (shelled or unshelled)
- ✓ Preferably Spanish extra virgin olive oil!
- ✓ One tablespoon minced garlic each person, less or more depending on your garlic love
- ✓ A little dry sherry I prefer fino or manzanilla (this can be omitted or substituted for a very dry white wine)
- ✓ A dash of butter on each plate
- ✓ 1-2 small cayenne peppers
- ✓ SEA SALT

Instructions

1. My mother-in-law prepares these in individual clay plates (cazuelitas) that may be cooked directly on the burner. Here, I'm assuming that most

people will prepare the dish in one colossal pan and then plate it separately.

2. Remove the shells from the shrimp if they have not been shelled.

3. Cover the bottom of a large frying pan with olive oil and heat slowly while adding the garlic and cayenne pepper pods.

4.

Add the shrimp and sauté for a moment until the garlic begins to crackle.

5. Add a splash of sherry and a sprinkling of salt once everything begins to sizzle again.

6. Simmer for approximately one minute, or until the opaque shrimp (do not overcook!)

7. Take the pan from the heat and divide the mixture into four servings.

8. Before serving, drizzle a touch of butter over each portion and give it a little swirl.

Notes

1. If possible, serve sizzling and crusty bread to soak up the sauce. Remember to cook the shrimp for approximately one minute; they can quickly overcook and continue to cook if left in the same dish once removed from the heat!

2. Bear in mind that olive oil plays a significant role in this recipe, so use the best quality extra virgin olive oil you can find!

Perfect Boiled Shrimp

Cook Time: 5 minutes

Total Time: 5 minutes

Servings: 4 servings

Ingredients

- ✓ 2 lb 1 kg raw shrimp (prawns), gambas y langostinos (shrimp and gumbo shrimp)!
- ✓ Water Pay attention to the quantity!
- ✓ 2 cups ice
- ✓ 4 tbsp sea salt
- ✓ slit spoon

Instructions

1. First, prepare the water bath by filling a large bowl halfway with cold water and adding ice and sea salt. Stir the mixture vigorously until the water is ice cold and the salt has dissolved.

2. Add 4-5 quarts of water and heat to a rolling boil in a big pot.

3. Stir in all the shrimp at once.

4. Adding the shrimp will bring the water back to a boil for about a minute; when the water returns to a spot and the shrimp change color and begin to float to the top, remove them immediately—do not overcook!

5. Quickly remove them and place them directly into the cold water basin using a slotted spoon. Even after adding all the hot shrimp, the water should remain cold; add more ice!

6. After 15 minutes, rinse the shrimp and serve immediately or cover with a damp paper towel and store in the refrigerator for up to one day.

7. In Spain, we serve the dish plain, occasionally with sliced lemon. They are peeled by hand and do not require deveining. You may shell and devein before serving if you choose, but it is not necessary!

Spanish Fried Anchovies

Prep Time: 5 minutes

Cook Time: 15 minutes

Servings: 4

Ingredients

- ✓ 1 lb fresh anchovies
- ✓ 1 c white flour
- ✓ 1 tbsp salt
- ✓ frying olive oil
- ✓ serve lemon wedges

Instructions

1. To begin, clean and fillet the anchovies. Remove the heads, and then clean out the insides of the fish with your thumb. Ensure that the spine is removed. Rinse and dry the fish in cold water. * In Spain, we frequently retain the spine and consume it for the calcium and crunch. You are welcome to do the same with your anchovies if they are small enough!

2. In a large mixing bowl, blend the flour and salt using your hands. Roll the anchovies in the flour mixture one time, coating evenly on all sides.

3. Heat olive oil to a depth of half an inch in a medium-sized skillet over medium heat. Before the oil begins to smoke (or shines), start frying the anchovies in small batches, not to overcrowd the pan. Cook until both sides are golden brown. approximately 1 minute per side.

4. Using a slotted spoon, remove the foil and set it on a dish lined with paper towels.

5. a teaspoon of salt and lemon wedges

Spanish Clams with Chorizo in Garlic Sauce

Prep Time: 10 minutes

Cook Time: 20 minutes

Servings: 4 servings

Ingredients

- ✓ 2 tbsp olive
- ✓ One medium onion, diced
- ✓ 1/2 pound semi-cured chorizo, sliced 1/4"
- ✓ Eight garlic cloves diced
- ✓ 1 tsp smoked paprika
- ✓ White wine 3 c
- ✓ 6 pounds littleneck clams washed
- ✓ 1/2 c. fresh parsley
- ✓ 2Tbsp butter

Instructions

1. Heat olive oil in a big saucepan. Until tender and translucent, sauté onion in hot oil. (Approximately 3-4 minutes). Add the chorizo to the pan and cook for an additional 3 minutes, or until enough fat has been rendered to coat the onion thoroughly.

2. Then add the garlic and paprika. Stir and continue sauteing for a further minute, or until aromatic.

3. Fill the pot halfway with white wine. Add the clams and bring to a boil. Evenly distribute the clams throughout the saucepan. Cook, covered, for 6-7 minutes, or until the clams open. Non-openers should be discarded.

4. Then add the parsley and butter. Hot with fresh bread and salt and pepper to taste.

Spanish Shrimp Fritters

Prep Time: 1 hour

Cook Time: 20 minutes

Total Time: 1 hour 20 minutes

Servings: 4 servings

Ingredients

- ✓ 150g Camarones baby shrimp
- ✓ 3/4 cup flour
- ✓ 3/4 cup chickpea
- ✓ 1 cup ice water
- ✓ One finely diced spring onion
- ✓ Good Spanish olive oil
- ✓ Fresh chopped parsley

Instructions

1. Combine the flour, chickpea flour, diced onion, chopped parsley, and a touch of salt in a mixing bowl.

2. Stir in the glass of water until a smooth batter with a runny consistency form.

3. Stir in the shrimp until completely coated in the batter. Allow 30 minutes for the mixture to chill in the refrigerator (this will aid in achieving the ultimate crispiness in the patties!).

4. Heat olive oil to a depth of about 2 centimeters in a big, shallow frying pan (just below an inch). Heat over somewhat high heat.

5. Once the oil has heated to the proper temperature, begin adding tablespoons of the batter to the frying pan. The batter should bubble and crisp up into fritters. Add enough patties to fill the pan without allowing them to contact one another or the frying pan's edges.

6. Fry until golden brown, rotating halfway through to ensure both sides are crisp.

7. When ready, remove the patties from the pan with tongs, allowing any remaining oil to drop back into the pan. Place carefully on a paper towel-lined platter.

8. Serve immediately, seasoning with additional salt if desired.

Fried Calamari Recipe

Prep Time: 30 minutes

Cook Time: 10 minutes

Total Time: 40 minutes

Servings: 4 servings

Ingredients

- ✓ 1 pound cleaned and ringed squid
- ✓ One lemon or enough milk to completely cover the squid
- ✓ 2 cup all-purpose flour (240 g)
- ✓ 1/2 tsp smoked paprika (2.5 g)
- ✓ 1/2 tsp black pepper (2.5 g)
- ✓ 1 tsp salt
- ✓ 1/2 cup whole milk (120 ml)

- ✓ 2 cups olive oil or enough to fry in your pan
- ✓ One lemon, split into wedges

Instructions

1. The first step is to slice the cleaned squid into rings approximately a half-inch thick. Transfer the mixture to a mixing bowl and add the lemon juice or milk. Although I prefer the milk technique, you can substitute any liquid on hand. Allow 30 minutes for the squid to tenderize.

2. In the meantime, whisk together the flour, paprika, salt, and black pepper in a bowl. Half of the mixture should be transferred to a second bowl. Transfer 1/2 cup milk to a third bowl.

3. When the squid is tender, drain the liquid. Using paper towels, pat the squid dry. You don't want to add more moisture.

4. Heat a large skillet over medium-high heat and add the olive oil until it reaches a depth of slightly more than half an inch.

5. Once the oil is heated, prepare the squid one piece by immersing it in the first bowl of the flour mixture, then in the milk bowl, and finally in the second dish of the flour mixture.

6. Fry in batches (avoid crowding the pan) for 2-3 minutes, or until golden brown on both sides.

7. Serve immediately with lemon wedges or homemade aioli.

Notes

1. For exceptionally tender calamari, marinate the squid for at least 30 minutes in milk or lemon juice before frying. If using milk, marinate for

many hours or overnight before serving. Limit the time with lemon juice to 30 minutes or cook due to the acid.

2. To make fried calamari gluten-free, simply use chickpea (garbanzo) flour. They're delectable!

3. You may use frozen calamari rings if you thaw them first and pat them dry with paper towels.

4. While these are best served immediately, they can be stored in the refrigerator for two days. Refrigerate and reheat in a hot oven for a few minutes.

Tuna Stuffed Piquillo Peppers

Prep Time: 15 minutes

Total Time: 15 minutes

Servings: 12 pintxos

Ingredients

- ✓ One can drained tuna drained
- ✓ One c. mayonnaise
- ✓ 4 tbsp chopped flat-leaf parsley
- ✓ One finely diced shallot
- ✓ 1 tsp lemon juice
- ✓ 1/4 cup Oil
- ✓ 1 tsp salt
- ✓ PEPPER TO TASTE
- ✓ One jar roasted piquillo peppers (12 peppers)
- ✓ 12 thick baguette slices 1" thick

Instructions

1.Heat oven to 325F (160C) and line a baking pan with baguette pieces.

2. Bake for 6-8 minutes, or until lightly browned the bread. Take the oven out of the range.

3. Combine 1/4 cup mayonnaise, tuna, shallot, lemon juice, olive oil, salt, and half of the parsley in a large mixing dish. Combine all ingredients and taste. Season with salt, pepper, lemon juice, and oil to taste.

4. Stuff the tuna mixture into each piquillo pepper, careful not to damage them. Take care not to overfill them!

5. Arrange each tuna-stuffed pepper on a toasted slice of bread and drizzle with extra virgin olive oil. Add mayonnaise and parsley to taste, if desired. Serve right away.

Watermelon Mint Gazpacho Recipe

Prep Time: 10 minutes

Cook Time: 10 minutes

Total Time: 20 minutes

Servings: 4 glasses

Ingredients

✓ Three oversized, ripe tomatoes, roughly sliced

✓ 3 inches mild green pepper, chopped

✓ One tiny garlic clove, cut into pieces

✓ 1/2 tiny chopped onion

✓ A good watermelon makes a good gazpacho, so use it!

✓ Salt to taste

- ✓ 1/4 cup oil
- ✓ Two teaspoons sherry vinegar
- ✓ A handful of fresh mint

Instructions

1. Prepare the tomatoes, pepper, and onion by washing and chopping them. Use only the freshest fruits and vegetables possible—gazpacho is a raw meal.

2. Puree the tomatoes, green pepper, onion, and garlic in a blender until smooth.

3. Drain the vegetable liquid in a fine mesh strainer.

4. Everything but a layer of seeds and skin should pass through. This should be discarded.

5. Reintroduce the vegetable juice to the blender along with the watermelon. Continue blending until thoroughly pureed.

6. Blend in salt to taste (start light; you can always add more afterward) and a couple of dashes of vinegar. Because everyone's choice for the amount of vinegar to add varies, I advise starting with a teaspoon or two and modifying as needed.

7. Finally, slowly add the extra virgin olive oil (better olive oil equals better gazpacho) while the blender is running.

8. Adjust the salt and vinegar to taste in the gazpacho. Then, add two to four ice cubes (depending on how thin you like your gazpacho). Allow them to melt in the blender for a few minutes before adding a handful of fresh mint and blending one final time.

9. Salt and pepper to taste in glasses. If serving in a bowl, garnish with chopped watermelon or red bell pepper.

Green Gazpacho Recipe

Prep Time: 5 minutes

Cook Time: 5 minutes

Total Time: 10 minutes

Servings: 4 servings

Ingredients

- ✓ 4-6 medium green tomatoes, chopped (be sure to use green tomatoes, and not unripe ones)
- ✓ One small-seeded and sliced cucumber
- ✓ 1/2 green bell pepper, diced
- ✓ 1/2 small white onion, diced
- ✓ One garlic clove
- ✓ 1/2 medium avocado make it ripe
- ✓ 1/2 cup chopped parsley
- ✓ 1 cup chopped mint
- ✓ Start with a hefty pinch of salt.
- ✓ Two tablespoons sherry vinegar (add more towards the end)
- ✓ 1 tsp lemon juice to prevent browning
- ✓ 1/2 cup Oil
- ✓ 1/4 cup spinach (optional) – but adds color to the gazpacho green color

Instructions

1. In a blender, combine the vegetables (excluding the avocado and herbs).
2. Add the tablespoon of lemon juice.

2. Pulse several times and then blend on high speed for several minutes or thoroughly pureed.

3. Combine the avocado, herbs, salt, and sherry vinegar in a blender.

4. Blend in the olive oil slowly at low speed.

5. Stir in the spinach to add a pop of green color (optional)

6. Adjust seasoning with salt and vinegar to taste. If the gazpacho is excessively thick, thin it out with a tablespoon of ice-cold water. Strain if desired for a smoother texture.

7. Enjoy!

Cold Beet Soup Recipe

Prep Time: 10 minutes

Cook Time: 10 minutes

Total Time: 20 minutes

Servings: 4 servings

Ingredients

- ✓ 2-3 big beets cooked (liquid reserved)
- ✓ 2-3 small plum tomatoes, chopped
- ✓ 1/2 cup Oil
- ✓ 1 tsp sherry vinegar
- ✓ 1.5 cups bread guts (the inside of a substantial bread, not the crust)
- ✓ One orange juice
- ✓ 2 tsp salt

Toppings

- ✓ Calamari smoke
- ✓ olives
- ✓ feta cheese
- ✓ Apple diced

✓ sliced orange

Instructions

1. Boil the beets until tender. Remove and allow it to cool somewhat before reserving the cooking water.

2. In a blender, combine the beets, 1/4 cup cooking water, fresh orange juice, sherry vinegar, tomatoes, and a pinch of salt. Pulse a few times to coarsely combine.

3. Stir in the bread to this mixture. Allow 5 minutes before blending on high speed until smooth. The consistency should be thick like a smoothie. If the surface is more ice cream-like (too thick), add a bit more cooking liquid to thin it out.

4. Now, mix on medium speed while slowly adding the olive oil. When thoroughly combined, taste and season with salt. If it's still too thick, add more cooking liquid.

5. Chill thoroughly (in the refrigerator, 2-4 hours) before serving. This can be eaten plain or with any of the toppings listed above. Enjoy!

Chilled Almond Soup

Prep Time: 5 minutes

Cook Time: 5 minutes

Total Time: 10 minutes

Servings: 4 -6 servings

Ingredients

✓ 1 cup blanched Marcona almonds, strained

✓ Two cubes of dried white bread

- ✓ One small garlic clove, remove the green germ
- ✓ 1-2 teaspoons sherry vinegar, to taste
- ✓ One peeled and diced apple (something tart and juicy like a Granny Smith or Pink Lady works well)
- ✓ SALT TO TASTE
- ✓ 1 cup cold water
- ✓ Ice cubes if time is short
- ✓ 1/4 cup extra virgin olive
- ✓ Green grapes

Instructions

1. Fill the blender halfway with stale bread and half with cold water and vinegar.
2. Combine the strained almonds, diced apple, and garlic in a medium bowl.
3. In a blender, pulse until smooth.
4. Adjust seasonings with salt and vinegar to taste.
5. If serving immediately, add ice (to ensure the drink is thoroughly cooled).
6. Slowly add the olive oil while mixing.
7. Season to taste and make any adjustments
8. If you have time, chill in the refrigerator.
9. To serve, scatter sliced green grapes on top.

RED BELL PEPPER TAPAS

READY IN: 2hrs

SERVES: 6

INGREDIENTS

- ✓ One minced garlic clove
- ✓ 1/2 teaspoon dry oregano or one teaspoon fresh oregano
- ✓ 2 tbsp olive oil
- ✓ Two red peppers

DIRECTIONS

1. Position broiler rack within a 4-inch radius of the heat source.
2. Preheat the broiler and cover the broiler pan with foil.
3. Arrange peppers on a sheet of heated foil.
4. Broil for 15-20 minutes, rotating every 5 minutes, until the skin is browned.
5. Remove broiler and place peppers in a brown paper bag.
6. Roll the top of the bag down and leave aside for 15 minutes; this steams the skins, making them easier to remove.
7. Peel peppers by cutting around and twisting the stem halves them, then peeling back the skin with a knife.
8. Rinse peppers under cold running water and discard seeds.
9. Cut pepper halves in half lengthwise and then into 1/4 inch strips.
10. Fill a jar halfway with pepper strips.
11. Combine the oregano, garlic, and oil.
12. Replace the top and shake vigorously to combine.
13. Allow an hour for marinating.
14. We enjoy this with garlic toast.
15. This will keep in the refrigerator for one week in a jar.
16. I haven't tried marinating it for that long, but I'm sure it would be delicious.

17.   Steaming and marinating time are included in the cooking time.

GAMBAS AL AJILLO GARLIC SHRIMP TAPAS

READY IN: 15mins

SERVES: 4

INGREDIENTS

- ✓ 1/4 CUP Oil
- ✓ Two fresh freshly chopped jalapenos or three minced jalapeño peppers
- ✓ Three garlic cloves, chopped
- ✓ Eight oz. chopped fresh shrimp
- ✓ 3 tbsp cilantro, chopped
- ✓ 1/2 tsp paprika (Hot Hungarian is best)
- ✓ salt
- ✓ 16 baguette slices

DIRECTIONS

1. Heat the oil in a skillet and add the jalapeño and garlic; cook for 1 minute.
2. Cook for 2 minutes with shrimp.
3. Add cilantro, paprika, and salt and heat through.
4. Bring the skillet, bread, and four spoons to the table. Each person fixes their own, and they get to soak any remaining scraps of bread.

ORANGE AND LEMON SAUCE

READY IN: 20mins

SERVES: 4

INGREDIENTS

- ✓ 1 (15 oz) white asparagus can (or green)

SAUCE

- ✓ Two hard-boiled egg yolks
- ✓ Two egg yolk
- ✓ 1 tsp lemon juice
- ✓ 1 tsp orange juice
- ✓ 1 tsp salt and pepper
- ✓ 1/2c olive oil
- ✓ 1egg white
- ✓ 1orange, cut
- ✓ 1lemon slices

DIRECTIONS

1. In a sieve, drain the asparagus.

2. Chop the hard-boiled egg yolks into small pieces and combine them with the raw egg yolk.

3. Add salt, pepper, and orange and lemon juices.

4. Add the olive oil gradually, pounding as though making mayonnaise.

5. Season to taste.

6. Add the egg whites to the sauce after beating until stiff.

7. Arrange the well-drained asparagus on a serving dish, drizzle with sauce, and garnish with orange and lemon slices.

TAPAS GARLIC MUSHROOMS

SERVES: 4

INGREDIENTS

- ✓ 1/4 cup oil
- ✓ Three minced garlic
- ✓ 2/3lb fresh white button mushrooms, cleaned
- ✓ Kosher salt
- ✓ Freshly ground black pepper
- ✓ Two teaspoons dry fino or oloroso sherry

DIRECTIONS

1. Heat olive oil and add garlic in a heavy skillet over medium-low heat. Cook, sometimes turning, until garlic is tender but not browned.

2. Add salt, pepper, and mushrooms. Whisk in the garlic and spices over medium-high heat. Cook, occasionally stirring, until the liquid from the mushrooms has evaporated and the mushrooms begin to brown, about six minutes.

3. Boost the heat and sherry, and simmer, constantly stirring, until the mushrooms are brown and the wine has evaporated.

4. Serve immediately, with salt and pepper.

MUSHROOMS AND ALIOLI TAPAS

READY IN: 25mins

SERVES: 10-12

INGREDIENTS

- ✓ 4 – 5 oz. sliced thin mushrooms

- ✓ 1 tsp extra virgin olive
- ✓ 1 tsp salt
- ✓ 1 tsp sherry
- ✓ garlic mayo (aioli)
- ✓ French bread, sliced

DIRECTIONS

1. In a saucepan, heat the olive oil. Add the mushrooms, salt, and sharry to the heated oil. Cover and turn heat down. Cook for around 10 minutes, or until liquid is released from the mushrooms. Drain and reserve.
2. Toast bread briefly to slightly dry it out.
3. Spread aioli on toast and top with mushrooms.
4. Broil for approximately 30 seconds or until the aioli begins to bubble.
5. Serve immediately.

TOMATES RELLENOS - TAPAS

READY IN: 30mins

SERVES: 6

INGREDIENTS

- ✓ Six tomatoes
- ✓ 3-hardboiled eggs-mashed
- ✓ 4 tbsp aioli (or mayonnaise)
- ✓ seasoning
- ✓ 1 tsp chopped parsley
- ✓ olive oil

DIRECTIONS

1. Remove the tops and sometimes a slice from the bottoms of the tomatoes to allow them to stand flat.

2. Using a spoon or knife, scrape the insides of the tomatoes.

3. Combine the eggs, aioli, salt, pepper, and parsley in a mixing bowl.

4. Fill the tomatoes halfway. Replace the tops and season with olive oil and freshly ground black pepper.

5. Suggestions: If the mixture appears too soft, add additional bread crumbs. Suppose you're not using aioli, season mayonnaise with garlic.

SETAS - WILD MUSHROOM AND GARLIC TAPAS

READY IN: 20mins

SERVES: 2

INGREDIENTS

- ✓ Four clove garlic
- ✓ 3 tbsp olive oil
- ✓ 1/2.kg wild mushroom (setas)
- ✓ 1/2 c white wine
- ✓ Three parsley
- ✓ salt
- ✓ pepper (optional)

DIRECTIONS

1. Begin by adequately washing the mushrooms, then placing them in a colander and allowing them to dry for a few minutes - if you need to cook them immediately, pat them dry with a tea towel. You may just tear the

mushrooms into strips if you use the type I used, but you must slice them with a knife if you use button mushrooms.

2. Heat all the oil in a frying pan until it begins to smoke. Stir in the garlic, which has been peeled and cut coarsely, using a wooden spoon. When the garlic starts to brown, add the mushrooms and cook, occasionally stirring, for 5 minutes. Add the wine and reduce to medium heat. Add the parsley and serve immediately after another 5 to 10 minutes.

MARINATED GREEN OLIVES (TAPAS)

READY IN: 10mins

SERVES: 8

YIELD: 1 lb olives

INGREDIENTS

- ✓ 1 pound olives
- ✓ Six chopped garlic
- ✓ 1 tsp crushed coriander
- ✓ 1 tsp crushed fennel
- ✓ Six thyme sprigs
- ✓ 2rosemary sprig
- ✓ One orange, zest, juice,
- ✓ One olive oil

DIRECTIONS

1. In a bowl, place the olives.

2. Combine the garlic, coriander, fennel, thyme, rosemary, orange zest, and orange juice in a jar large enough to hold them all (and that had a lid that tightly closed).

3. Pour in enough olive oil to completely cover the olives.

4. Shake thoroughly and marinate for six days at room temperature.

STUFFED CHERRY TOMATO TAPAS

READY IN: 15mins

YIELD: 24 tapas

INGREDIENTS

- ✓ 3 oz Pimento olives (Spanish)
- ✓ 1 tbsp drained capers
- ✓ 1tsp brandy
- ✓ 1/4 tsp lemon zest
- ✓ Two tablespoons extra virgin olive oil
- ✓ 24 cherry Tomatoes
- ✓ chopped parsley (to garnish)

DIRECTIONS

1. Process the olives until coarsely chopped in a food processor.

2. Process the remaining ingredients for the tapenade until the olives are minced.

3. Remove a thin slice from the top and bottom of each tomato with a sharp knife and discard.

4. Scoop the juice and seeds from each tomato, leaving the shells intact, and pour some tapenade into each shell.

5. Garnish with parsley and serve, if desired. Serve at room temperature.

GRILLED GOAT'S CHEESE ON A BED OF LETTUCE

READY IN: 20mins

SERVES: 4-6

INGREDIENTS

- ✓ 11 oz goat cheese
- ✓ 1 tsp oil
- ✓ 4 cups Baby Spinach

VINAIGRETTE

- ✓ 1/2 virgin olive oil
- ✓ 3 tbsp sherry vinegar
- ✓ 1 tsp honey
- ✓ Salt

DIRECTIONS

1. Preheat oven to grill mode.

Vinaigrette:

1. In a small bowl, dissolve the salt, pepper, and honey in the vinegar. Add the virgin olive oil and whisk until an emulsion forms.
2. Slice the cheese 3/4 inch thick and cook until brown in the oven.
3. Arrange baby greens on plates, drizzle with vinaigrette, and top with cheese.

TAPAS - SHRIMP IN GREEN MAYO

READY IN: 5mins

SERVES: 10

INGREDIENTS

- ✓ 1/2 cup mayonnaise
- ✓ 1/4c parsley mince
- ✓ 2 tsp coarsely chopped capers
- ✓ 1/4 tsp dried oregano
- ✓ One clove minced garlic
- ✓ 1lb shrimp cooked, peeled & deveined (30 - 40)

DIRECTIONS

1. In a medium-sized serving bowl, combine the first five ingredients.
2. Add shrimp and gently toss until well combined.
3. Chill until ready to serve.

SHRIMP AND POTATO TAPAS WW CORE POINTS

READY IN: 40mins

SERVES: 6

INGREDIENTS

- ✓ 1 pound red potatoes, sliced in half
- ✓ 2 tbsp olive oil
- ✓ 1 lb medium shrimp, deveined and halved
- ✓ 4 Garlic, minced
- ✓ 1 1/2 tbsp white wine vinegar
- ✓ 1/2 teaspoon red pepper flakes
- ✓ 1/2 tsp salt

DIRECTIONS

1. In a large saucepan, combine the potatoes and enough water to cover. Bring to a boil—Cook for approximately 7 minutes or until fork-tender. Drain and set aside for 5 minutes to cool.

2. In a large nonstick skillet, heat oil over medium-high heat. Cook, shaking the pan regularly until the potatoes are browned and crisp, about 5 minutes.

3. Add the shrimp and garlic and simmer, turning regularly, for about 2 minutes, or until the shrimp are opaque in the center. Combine vinegar, pepper, and salt.

MUSHROOM TOAST TAPAS

READY IN: 35mins

SERVES: 8

INGREDIENTS

- ✓ 1 tbsp olive oil
- ✓ 1/2 lb mushroom, cleaned, brushed, and cut
- ✓ One clove minced garlic
- ✓ 1 tsp minced parsley
- ✓ salt & freshly ground black pepper
- ✓ 2 tbsp grated manchego or parmesan
- ✓ Eight sandwich bread slices (crust removed)

WHITE SAUCE

- ✓ 3 tbsp butter
- ✓ 3 tbsp all-purpose flour
- ✓ 3tablespoons milk plus

- ✓ 1/2 cup milk
- ✓ 1 tsp white wine
- ✓ salt and freshly ground black pepper
- ✓ Nutmeg (be generous)
- ✓ cayenne (be generous)

DIRECTIONS

1. Prepare the white sauce by melting the butter in a skillet over low to medium heat and whisking in the flour.
2. Cook and stir for a few minutes longer, then gradually add the milk and wine and cook, continually stirring, until thickened and smooth.
3. Season with salt, pepper, nutmeg (to taste), and cayenne pepper (to taste); while it is recommended to be generous with the cayenne and nutmeg, this is entirely up to you.
4. Take the pan off the heat and set it aside.
5. Heat the oil in a skillet until very hot; add the mushrooms and saute for about 2 minutes over high heat.
6. (I added the dried parsley approximately 1 minute into the cooking time; if using fresh parsley, proceed to the following step.) If the mushrooms release liquid, simmer until it has evaporated before proceeding.
7. Turn off the fire and add the garlic, parsley (if not already added), ham, salt, and pepper.
8. Combine with the white sauce and toss in the cheese until smooth and all ingredients are spread equally.

9. To this point, the mixture may be prepared ahead of time and refrigerated.

10. To begin, lightly toast the bread and cut each slice into two triangles.

11. 11.1/8 of the mushroom mixture should thoroughly cover each triangle.

12. You may prepare this in various ways: broil until brown, fry face down in 1/2 inch of heated oil, or encase in puff pastry dough.

13. If using puff pastry dough, you will need around 1 pound; cut the crust into three-inch strips and wrap them about two tablespoons of filling.

14. Bake for 8 minutes at 400 degrees.

15. The filling can also be used to fill miniature pastry puff tart shells.

SARDINE TAPAS

READY IN: 10mins

SERVES: 4

INGREDIENTS

- ✓ 12 cup Olive oil
- ✓ self-rising flour
- ✓ 3/4lb sardine
- ✓ SALT (sea salt is recommended)
- ✓ a lemon (to garnish)

DIRECTIONS

1. In a skillet, heat the oil.
2. Coat the sardines with flour.

3. Cook, occasionally stirring, until golden brown and heated through.

4. Carefully remove from pan, drain, and season with salt.

5. Garnish with wedges of lemon.

BREAD AND CHOCOLATE TAPAS -- PAN Y CHOCOLATE

READY IN: 10mins

SERVES: 4-5

INGREDIENTS

- ✓ Ten slices baguette
- ✓ 3 oz. bittersweet chocolate
- ✓ 3-4 tsp extra virgin olive oil
- ✓ salt to taste

DIRECTIONS

1. Preheat oven broiler to high.

2. Broil the bread on a cookie sheet until browned.

3. Remove the baking sheet from the oven.

4. Preheat oven to 350 degrees F.

5. In the meantime, sprinkle oil over each baguette slice.

6. Season with a pinch of salt.

7. Spread a little chocolate on each one.

8. Bake for 5 minutes or until the chocolate is completely melted.

9. Serve immediately.

SHRIMP WITH SPICY SAFFRON SAUCE (TAPAS)FR

READY IN: 4mins

SERVES: 4

INGREDIENTS

- ✓ 1/8 teaspoon saffron threads or turmeric
- ✓ 2 tbsp Duke's or Hellmann's mayonnaise
- ✓ Eight deveined jumbo shrimp
- ✓ One shallot
- ✓ One minced garlic clove
- ✓ 2 tsp canola oil
- ✓ 1/2 lemon zest
- ✓ One small baguette or one tiny pita bread

DIRECTIONS

1. Whisk together 1/8 teaspoon saffron threads or turmeric and mayonnaise in a small dish.
2. Made apart for marriage.
3. Before browning, sauté garlic and shallot in canola oil in a skillet.
4. Add shrimp and heat until they begin to turn pink.
5. Garnish with Saffron/Turmeric Aioli and petite baguette or pita rounds.

TUNA STUFFED PIQUILLO PEPPERS TAPAS

READY IN: 20mins

SERVES: 8

INGREDIENTS

- ✓ piquillo pepper, drained
- ✓ 2 (7 oz) cans tuna with olive oil
- ✓ Four chopped green onions

- ✓ 1/4 cup chopped parsley
- ✓ 1 tsp sherry wine vinegar
- ✓ One minced garlic clove
- ✓ 1/2cup black olive, chopped
- ✓ One boiled egg, diced
- ✓ 1/2teaspoon sweet smoked paprika

DIRECTIONS

1. Drain and flake tuna using a fork.
2. Gently combine all ingredients except peppers into tuna.
3. Fill peppers halfway with tuna mixture. Refrigerate for 20 minutes.
4. Refrigerate until serving.
5. To prepare the egg, place it in a saucepan of cold water over high heat when it reaches a boil, cover, and remove it from heat. Allow ten minutes—peel under running cold water.

PEARL ONION TAPAS

READY IN: 1hr

SERVES: 8-10

INGREDIENTS

- ✓ 1 pound pearl onions or shallots
- ✓ 6 tsp olive oil
- ✓ 7 oz. sherry vinegar
- ✓ 3-4 oz sherry wine
- ✓ 2thyme sprigs
- ✓ salt and pepper

✓ 1 tsp sugar

DIRECTIONS

1. Remove the pearl onion's peel.

2. In a saute pan, heat the oil. Cook the onion over medium heat. Sauté until a pale golden hue develops.

3. Sprinkle sugar over onions and cook for about a minute until caramelized.

4. Combine sherry vinegar and sherry in a small bowl. Add the thyme twigs and season with salt and pepper to taste.

5. 30 minutes covered on low heat

6. Allow cooling slightly before serving in tiny bowls.

PIMENTOS DE PADRON TAPAS

READY IN: 10mins

SERVES: 4

INGREDIENTS

✓ 20-40 Padron peppers

✓ 1/2 CUP Olive oil

✓ 1 -3 garlic cloves, minced (to your taste)

✓ salt (to your taste)

✓ Vinegar balsamic (optional, to your taste)

DIRECTIONS

1. Rinse and pat dry peppers.

2. Large skillet with olive oil

3. Fry and stir peppers vigorously for approximately 3 minutes, or until blistered and burst.

4. Drain peppers from oil and place them on a paper towel-lined platter to dry.

5. Season generously with sea salt and garlic powder and serve!

6. While garlic is not traditionally served, it adds an extra spice that I appreciate.

7. I have also poured a tiny bit of excellent quality balsamic vinegar or red pepper flakes on the peppers for a zesty flavor.

CHICKEN WITH LEMON AND GARLIC TAPAS

READY IN: 20mins

SERVES: 4

INGREDIENTS

- ✓ 8 oz skinless chicken breast fillets
- ✓ 2 tbsp olive oil
- ✓ 1shallot
- ✓ 1/4 tsp garlic
- ✓ 1 tsp paprika
- ✓ One lemon, juiced
- ✓ One lemon, sliced (garnish)
- ✓ salt
- ✓ pepper
- ✓ 2 tsp chopped parsley
- ✓ Parsley, stem, one sprig (garnish)

DIRECTIONS

1. Sandwich the chicken breast fillets between two sheets of clear plastic wrap (plastic wrap) or parchment paper. Roll out the fillets with a rolling pin or meat mallet until they are approximately 1/4 inch thick.

2. Using a sharp knife, cut the chicken into 1/2-inch broad strips.

3. In a big, heavy frying pan or wok, heat the oil until extraordinarily high but not smoking. Stir-fry the chicken strips, shallot, garlic, and paprika for approximately 3 minutes over high heat or until the chicken is cooked through.

4. Salt and pepper to taste and stir in the lemon juice and parsley. Garnish with lemon slices and serve warm. Garnish with a flat-leaf parsley stem.

CLAMS WITH GARLIC AND ALMONDS TAPAS

READY IN: 30mins

SERVES: 4

INGREDIENTS

- ✓ Album: 1lb littleneck clams
- ✓ 4 tbsp extra virgin olive
- ✓ Five garlic cloves, sliced
- ✓ 1 tsp blanched sliced almonds
- ✓ 2 c dry white wine (cava) (Spanish wine)
- ✓ Two lemons juice and zest
- ✓ 4scallions, finely sliced
- ✓ One bunch of chopped parsley

DIRECTIONS

1. Set aside cleaned and drained cockles.

2. Heat oil in a 12- to 14-inch frying pan until smoking.

3. Add the garlic and almonds and cook, frequently stirring, until golden brown. Bring clams, wine, lemon juice, and zest to a boil. Cook, covered, for approximately 3 to 4 minutes, or until clams open. Remove the lid, garnish with onions and parsley, and serve.

Spanish Garlic Shrimp

Prep: 15 mins

Cook: 5 mins

Total: 20 mins

Servings: 4

Yield: 1 pound of shrimp

Ingredients

- ✓ Four garlic cloves
- ✓ 1-lb thawed, peeled, and deveined large shrimp (21-25 count)
- ✓ kosher salt
- ✓ 1 tsp smoked paprika (optional)
- ✓ 1/4 c extra virgin olive
- ✓ 2 tsp dry sherry
- ✓ 1 tsp Parsley (Italian flat-leaf)

Directions

1. Garlic finely sliced Combine kosher salt and paprika in a small bowl. Coat with the mixture.

2. In a skillet over medium heat, saute the garlic and oil—Cook for approximately 2 minutes, or until the garlic begins to turn golden.

Increase heat to high and add shrimp. With tongs, toss and turn shrimp until they start to curl but remain uncooked, about 2 minutes. Add sherry. Cook, constantly stirring, for approximately 1 minute longer, until sauce comes to a boil and shrimp is cooked through. Take the pan off the heat. With a spoon, incorporate the parsley.

Avocado and Tuna Tapas

Prep: 20 mins

Total: 20 mins

Servings: 4

Yield: 4 servings

Ingredients

- ✓ Can solid white tuna (12 oz.)
- ✓ 2 tbsp mayonnaise
- ✓ Three green onions, thinly sliced
- ✓ 1/2 red bell peppers, diced
- ✓ 1 tsp balsamic vinegar
- ✓ a dash of cay
- ✓ 1 tsp garlic salt
- ✓ Two ripe avocados pitted

Directions

Combine the tuna, mayonnaise, green onions, red pepper, and balsamic vinegar in a bowl. Season with pepper and garlic salt, then spoon the tuna mixture into the avocado halves. Before serving, garnish with shaved green onions and a dash of black pepper.

Spanish Stuffed Olive Tapas with Feta

Prep: 30 mins

Cook: 3 mins

Additional: 8 hrs 15 mins

Total: 8 hrs 48 mins

Servings: 30

Yield: 30 servings

Ingredients

- ✓ 30 almonds blanched
- ✓ 1 (4 oz) feta crumble
- ✓ 1/2 minced onions
- ✓ Three minced garlic
- ✓ 1 tbsp extra virgin olive
- ✓ 30 ripe green olives

Directions

1. In a medium pan, toast almonds, turning regularly, for about 3 minutes, or until lightly toasted. Allow approximately 15 minutes for cooling.

2. In a small bowl, combine feta cheese, onion, and garlic. Combine with olive oil to form a homogeneous paste.

3. Spoon a small amount of feta paste into each olive and insert an almond. Halve huge almonds. Refrigerate for 8-12 hours. Serve the olives with toothpicks inserted into them.

Spanish Garlic Toast

Prep: 10 mins

Cook: 3 mins

Total: 13 mins

Servings: 6

Yield: 1 loaf

Ingredients

- ✓ 1 lb loaf thickly sliced
- ✓ Five garlic cloves, peeled
- ✓ One halved fresh tomato
- ✓ 1/4 cup extra virgin olive oil
- ✓ salt and pepper to taste

Directions

1. Preheat the oven's broiler and position the oven rack approximately 6 inches from the heat source.
2. 3–5 minutes to golden and crispy toast.
3. Rub toasted bread evenly with garlic cloves; rub with the cut side of tomato evenly. Use a pastry brush or your hands to spread olive oil evenly over the pieces—season with sea salt and freshly ground pepper.

Spanish Pan-Fried Shrimp with Garlic

Prep: 15 mins

Cook: 10 mins

Total: 25 mins

Servings: 4

Yield: 4 servings

Ingredients

- ✓ 1/2 cup olive oil
- ✓ One head garlic, peeled and chopped
- ✓ One dried red chile, seeds, and chopped
- ✓ 1 lb uncooked medium shrimp, deveined
- ✓ salt to taste
- ✓ Two teaspoons chopped fresh parsley

Directions

1. In a skillet over medium heat, heat 1/4 inch olive oil. Sauté garlic and chile pepper for about 1 minute, or until fragrant. Remove the garlic and chili peppers with a slotted spoon and set aside. To the hot oil, add shrimp—Cook and stir for approximately 3 minutes, or until the mixture is opaque in color.

2. Garlic and chile peppers should be returned to the skillet. Season with salt and continue cooking for an additional 2 minutes. Serve immediately garnished with fresh parsley.

MUSHROOM CROQUETTES

yield: 4

prep time: 3 HOURS

cook time: 15 MINUTES

total time: 3 HOURS 15 MINUTES

INGREDIENTS

- ✓ 1/4 cup olive oil, divided
- ✓ 1/2 chopped onion
- ✓ 2 minced garlic

- ✓ 215 g (7.5 oz) chopped mushrooms (I used wild, but any type will work: Portobello, oyster, Asian, button, cremini, etc.)
- ✓ 1/2 cup (75 g) flour
- ✓ 2 3/4 cup (650 milliliters) unsweetened plant-based milk
- ✓ 1/2 cup ml vegetable stock
- ✓ 1/2 tsp salt + extra for mushrooms
- ✓ PEPPER to taste
- ✓ 1 1/2 cups (135 g) bread crumb
- ✓ Fry-oil

INSTRUCTIONS

1. In a large skillet over medium heat, heat one tablespoon of oil. Cook until the onion is translucent, then add the garlic and cook until soft and fragrant. Transfer to a serving plate.

2. I usually cook the mushrooms in two batches, arranging them in a single layer in my pan and frying them rather than steaming them. Therefore, add half the chopped mushrooms and brown on the first side for a few minutes before stirring to brown on the second side. Season with salt and pepper and transfer to the plate with the onions while sautéing the second batch of mushrooms. Place aside.

3. Combine 1 3/4 cups (400 mL) of the plant milk with the vegetable stock in a measuring cup or bowl. Put aside for the time being.

4. In a small saucepan over medium heat, heat three tablespoons of olive oil. Sift in the flour gradually, stirring to ensure that it does not lump. You'll finish up with something resembling a dough ball. Allow it to

cook, stirring regularly, for a minute or two, or until the raw flour scent subsides.

5. Whisk in a bit of amount of the plant milk-stock mixture. At first, it will evaporate, but continue adding the liquid in tiny amounts, whisking continually until it becomes a sauce. To avoid lumps, whisk it vigorously! After all the milk is in, continue stirring as the mixture comes to a simmer and continue whisking for a couple more minutes, or until it reaches a thick consistency.

6. Remove from the fire and toss in the mushrooms, onion, and garlic, along with 12 tsp salt and freshly ground pepper to taste. Place the mixture in a serving dish to cool. Once cool, wrap it in plastic wrap, push the wrap against the top of the filling, and place it in the refrigerator until totally cold.

7. Heat oil for deep frying in a small saucepan over medium heat.

8. Combine the remaining cup (250 mL) of plant milk and the breadcrumbs in a separate bowl. Roll approximately a spoonful of the filling into a log shape. Cover it with breadcrumbs, then dip it in milk and then back into breadcrumbs.

9. Fry in groups of 5 or 6 until golden brown, flipping as necessary. Transfer to a plate lined with paper towels to drain.

10.   Serve.

Spanish Garlic Toast

Prep:10 mins

Cook:3 mins

Total:13 mins

Servings:6

Yield:1 loaf

Ingredients

- ✓ 1 lb loaf thickly sliced
- ✓ Five garlic cloves, peeled
- ✓ One halved fresh tomato
- ✓ 1/4 cup extra virgin olive oil
- ✓ salt and pepper to taste

Directions

1. Preheat the oven's broiler and position the oven rack approximately 6 inches from the heat source.
2. 3–5 minutes toast bread slices or brown and crunchy.
3. Rub toasted bread evenly with garlic cloves; rub with the cut side of tomato evenly. Use a pastry brush or your hands to spread olive oil evenly over the pieces—season with sea salt and freshly ground pepper.

Spanish Stuffed Olive Tapas with Feta

Prep: 30 mins

Cook: 3 mins

Additional: 8 hrs 15 mins

Total:8 hrs 48 mins

Servings: 30

Yield: 30 servings

Ingredients

- ✓ 30 almond blanched

- ✓ 1 (4 oz) feta crumble cheese
- ✓ 1/2 minced onion
- ✓ Three minced garlic cloves
- ✓ 1 tbsp extra virgin olive
- ✓ 30 green pitted olives

Directions

1. In a medium pan, toast almonds, turning regularly, for about 3 minutes, or until lightly toasted. Allow approximately 15 minutes for cooling.

2. In a small bowl, combine feta cheese, onion, and garlic. Combine with olive oil to form a homogeneous paste.

3. Spoon a small amount of feta paste into each olive and insert an almond. Halve huge almonds. Refrigerate for 8-12 hours. Serve the olives with toothpicks inserted into them.

Spanish Tortilla

Prep: 15 mins

Cook: 45 mins

Total: 1 hr

Servings6

Ingredients

- ✓ 750g Peeled potatoes, cut into 0.5cm (1/5") thick slices
- ✓ One chopped onion
- ✓ 125 ml olive oil
- ✓ Eight eggs
- ✓ SALT PEPPER

✓ Parsley

Instructions

1. In a nonstick frying pan over medium heat, heat the oil. Turn onion and potatoes over. Cover and gently simmer the potatoes for about 20 minutes, turning them three or four times with an egg flip until tender and cooked through. Reduce the heat if the potatoes begin to sizzle and brown.

2. In the meantime, whisk together eggs and season with salt and pepper.

3. When the potatoes are done, remove them with a slotted spatula and place them in a colander to drain any extra oil.

4. Pour away most of the remaining oil in the skillet, leaving around 1 1/2 – 2 tbsp.

5. Increase heat to medium-high. Increase the heat to high on the grill/broiler.

6. Add the potatoes back to the skillet and pour in the egg—Cook for 5 minutes, or until the underside is pale golden.

7. If the center of the omelet is still raw, as it usually always is, place it on the grill/broiler for a couple of minutes or until the center is just set.

8. Remove and set aside for a few moments. Place a serving tray on the frypan and flip it over to release the omelet.

9. Serve at room temperature or warm (I love warm!).

10. I included this in a Tapas Spread!

Stuffed cherry peppers

Prep:10 mins

Makes 20

Ingredients

- ✓ Three grilled artichokes (jarred)
- ✓ a rocket
- ✓ 2 tbsp feta crumbles
- ✓ 20 drained cherry peppers

Method

Artichokes and a handful of the rocket should be finely chopped. Combine with the crumbled feta cheese. Fill the pickled cherry peppers halfway with the mixture and serve.

Warm kale salad with almonds & Serrano ham

Prep:15 mins

Cook:20 mins

Serves 2 - 3

Ingredients

- ✓ Two banana shallots, sliced
- ✓ 2 tsp oil
- ✓ 200g Kale, big stems removed, leaves ripped
- ✓ 4-6 celery sticks, thinly sliced on an angle
- ✓ Three manchego cheese shavings (optional)

Dressing

- ✓ 2 tbsp sherry vinegar
- ✓ 2 tbsp olive oil
- ✓ 2 tsp Dijon mustard
- ✓ sugar pinch
- ✓ Two tbs raisins

Almonds

- ✓ 2 cup blanched almonds
- ✓ 1/2 tsp oil
- ✓ smoked paprika

Method

1. Preheat oven to 200°C/180°C fan/gas 6. 6. You are tossing the shallots with one teaspoon of oil on a large nonstick baking tray. As you flip the rings in the oil, gently separate them. Roast for 10 minutes, stirring halfway through, or until the vegetables begin to soften and become golden in spots.

2. Whisk together the vinegar, oil, mustard, sugar, and seasonings in a large basin to create the dressing. Stir in the raisins and set them aside to soak. Toss the almonds, oil, paprika, and a pinch of sea salt in a smaller roasting tin. Rub one teaspoon vegetable oil and seasoning all over the kale.

3. Remove the shallot tray from the oven, stir in the kale (it's okay if it mounds somewhat), then replace the tray in the range and place the almonds on the lower shelf. Roast for 7 minutes, turning halfway through until the kale is crisp in some spots and wilted in others.

4. Arrange the ham on serving plates in a ruffled pattern. Coat the kale, shallots, and celery in the dressing bowl, then mound on top of the ham and sprinkle with the almonds and cheese, if using.

Padron peppers

Cook:5 mins

Serves six as a side

Ingredients

- ✓ 1 tbsp olive oil
- ✓ 500g Padron peppers

Method

1. Heat the olive oil in a big frying pan. Stir constantly for 5 minutes, or until the peppers are blistered and wilted. Peppers should be slightly browned and tender.

2. Platter the peppers with olive oil. Season with sea salt. Serv as an accompaniment to dips or as part of a tapas dish.

Ham & cheese croquetas

Prep:20 mins

Cook:1 hr and 25 mins

plus 4 hrs 30 mins chilling

Makes 24

Ingredients

- ✓ 25 g butter
- ✓ 1/2 tiny sliced onion
- ✓ 50 g flour
- ✓ 250 ml milk
- ✓ 140g cubed smoked ham
- ✓ 50 g grated mature cheddar
- ✓ 50 g grated gruyère
- ✓ 1 tsp Dijon mustard

- ✓ 2 TBS double cream

Coating

- ✓ Two big eggs
- ✓ 50 g flour
- ✓ 140g dry bread crumbs
- ✓ deep-frying sunflower oil

Tomato Chilli Jam

- ✓ 300 g ripe tomatoes, chopped
- ✓ One finely chopped (deseeded if you don't like it hot)
- ✓ One red onion, diced
- ✓ Four big smashed garlic cloves
- ✓ 100g demerara sugar
- ✓ 100ml vinegar wine

Method

1. To prepare the croquetas, melt the butter in a medium skillet over medium heat and gently cook the onion for 3 minutes or lightly browned. Cook for 30 seconds while stirring in the flour. Add the milk gradually, stirring frequently, and simmer for 5 minutes, or until thick and glossy—season with salt and pepper to taste. Add ham, cheese, mustard, and cream. Cook for an additional minute, stirring regularly until the cheese melts.

2. Transfer to a dish and cover the surface with cling film to prevent the formation of skin. Allow to cool slightly before chilling for 4 hours or overnight - the mixture must be very stiff to create the croquetas. Take heaping teaspoons of the ingredients and roll them into 24 little oval

shapes using damp palms. Place on a tray. Whisk together the eggs, flour, and half of the breadcrumbs in a small dish.

3. Lightly coat each croqueta in flour, then in egg, and finally in breadcrumbs. Arrange on a baking sheet covered with parchment paper. Fill the bowl halfway through the coating process with the remaining breadcrumbs. Allow 30 minutes to chill (or to freeze, see tip, below left).

4. In the meantime, prepare the tomato chili jam. Bring all ingredients to a simmer in a big saucepan.Cook, covered lightly with a lid, for 50 minutes to 1 hour, until thick and glossy, stirring periodically. Allow cooling slightly before serving.

5. Half-fill a big saucepan with sunflower oil and heat to 180C. or heat the oil in an electric deep-fat fryer. Avoid overheating and leaving heated oil unattended. Drop six games of croquet into the oil using a metal slotted spoon and fry for 1.5 minutes or until golden brown. Transfer to a baking tray coated with kitchen paper to absorb any remaining oil and continue frying the remaining ingredients. Serve alongside the chili jam as a dipping sauce.

Andalusian-style chicken

Prep:10 mins

Cook:25 mins - 30 mins

Serves four as part of a tapas spread

Ingredients

- ✓ saffron pinch
- ✓ 120ml boiling water + 1/2 chicken stock cubes

- ✓ 2 tbsp olive
- ✓ One finely sliced onion
- ✓ Two large chicken breasts or six boneless, skinless thighs, diced
- ✓ a huge pinch of cinnamon
- ✓ One red chili, chopped
- ✓ 2 tbsp sherry
- ✓ 1 tbsp honey
- ✓ 6 quartered cherry tomatoes
- ✓ One tablespoons raisins
- ✓ coarsely chopped coriander
- ✓ 25 g pine nuts or almonds
- ✓ crusty bread

Method

1. Soak the saffron in the heated stock. In a medium saucepan, heat the oil and sauté the onion until tender and just beginning to turn brown. Add the chicken and push to the edge of the pan—Cook for a few minutes longer, or until the chicken is evenly browned.

2. Add cinnamon and chile after a few minutes. Combine the stock, vinegar, honey, tomatoes, and raisins in a medium bowl. Once boiling, decrease heat to low and simmer for 10 minutes, or until the sauce is reduced and the chicken is done. Sprinkle with coriander and almonds and serve alongside bread when ready to serve.

Clams with sherry & Serrano ham

Prep:5 mins

Cook:10 mins - 15 mins

Serves four as part of a tapas spread

Ingredients

- ✓ 1 tbsp olive
- ✓ 1/2 onion, finely chopped
- ✓ 500g clams
- ✓ 50 g serrano
- ✓ Two minced garlic cloves
- ✓ Sherry, 100ml
- ✓ Parsley, roughly sliced

Method

1. Heat the oil in a medium saucepan with a lid and sauté the onion for 5-7 minutes to soften. Rinse the clams in a colander and discard any that have been opened and cannot be closed with a sharp tap—Cook for 1 minute after adding the ham and garlic to the onion.

2. Add the clams and sherry to a saucepan and bring to a boil. Cover and cook for 4-5 minutes, or until all the clams have opened (discard any that haven't). Serve immediately with parsley sprinkled on top.

Ham & peach nibbles

Prep:15 mins

It makes 32 cocktail sticks

Ingredients

- ✓ Six ripe peaches
- ✓ a basil bunch

✓ serrano ham package

Method

Peaches should be sliced. Each peach slice should be wrapped with a basil leaf and a piece of Serrano ham and pierced with a short cocktail stick.

Sautéed chorizo with red wine

Prep:10 mins

Cook:15 mins - 20 mins

Serves 4

Ingredients

✓ 1 tbsp olive

✓ One chopped onion

✓ Two minced garlic cloves

✓ 500g chorizo, sliced into chunky pieces or left whole

✓ 100 ml red wine

✓ 1 tbsp honey

✓ chopped parsley

✓ serving bread

Method

1. Heat the oil in a large frying pan and gently sauté the onion for a few minutes or until softened. Cook for a few minutes with the garlic.

2. Remove the onion and garlic from the pan and add the chorizo. Brown evenly throughout, then add the wine and honey.

3. Cover and cook on low heat for 5 minutes, or until the sausages are cooked through and coated in sauce. If the pan appears dry, add water. Arrange parsley on top and some crusty bread on the side to mop up the spicy juices.

Smoky paprika peppers

Prep:10 mins

Cook:30 mins

It makes enough to fill 3 x 500ml jars

Ingredients

- ✓ 500ml olive oil
- ✓ 2 tsp smoked paprika
- ✓ One garlic clove, sliced
- ✓ black peppercorn one tsp
- ✓ One tablespoon fennel seed
- ✓ 8 Red peppers
- ✓ 8 Orange peppers
- ✓ flake salt
- ✓ 300ml vinegar wine
- ✓ flat-leaf parsley, chopped (optional)

Method

1. In a medium saucepan, pour the oil. Add the paprika and garlic and cook on low heat for 5 minutes, then set aside to cool. Strain through a muslin cloth over a sieve, removing the garlic and paprika to leave a bright

orange, fragrant oil. Dry-fry the spices for 1 minute in a separate pan to release their scents. Set aside the paprika oil.

2. Preheat the grill to a high setting. Cut the peppers in half (keep the stems – they'll quickly pull out afterward) and spread skin side up on two big baking pans—grill for approximately 15 minutes or until the skins are charred. Transfer the peppers, which are still hot, to plastic food bags, seal, and set aside to cool. Once the peppers have cooled sufficiently to handle, peel away the skins, pull out the stems, scoop out the seeds, and break into large pieces.

3. Bring the vinegar and 300ml water to a simmer in a large saucepan and add the peppers. Reintroduce to low heat for 3 minutes, then drain well and pack into jars or other heatproof containers. Reheat the spiced oil gently for a few minutes before pouring over the peppers and sealing. Add the parsley before serving the peppers (or immediately if using them the same day) since the parsley may discolor. Refrigerate for up to 1 week.

Flash-fried prawns with chili, lemon & parsley

Prep:10 mins

Cook:5 mins

Serves 6 - 8

Ingredients

- ✓ 2 tbsp Extra-virgin olive oil
- ✓ 300g raw butterflied prawn
- ✓ Two garlic cloves, thinly sliced
- ✓ 1 tsp chili flakes

- ✓ zing and Ju 1 lime
- ✓ 2 tsp parsley (chopped)

Method

1. Heat the olive oil in a big pan.Season the prawns with salt and pepper and put them aside. Cook the garlic over medium-low heat, occasionally stirring, until its color. Bring to high heat and add the prawns and chili. Stir briskly and turn the prawns in the pan often.

2. Add the lemon juice after 1 minute. Toss for an additional 1 minute or until prawns are opaque. Serve with crusty bread and lemon zest.

Crunchy baked mussels

Prep:25 mins

Cook:4 mins

Serves 4

Ingredients

- ✓ 1kg mussel shells
- ✓ 50g Toasted breadcrumb
- ✓ zest one lime
- ✓ 100 g garlic and parsley

Method

1. Scrub the mussels thoroughly and remove any beards. Rinse thoroughly with cold water and discard open, and do not close when tapped against the sink's side.

2. Drain the mussels and place them in a big saucepan along with a splash of water. Bring to a boil and then cover the pan, occasionally shaking, for

2-3 minutes, or until the mussels open. Drain thoroughly and then discard any that are still closed—Preheat grill to its highest setting.

3. Combine the crumbs and zest in a mixing bowl. Each mussel should have one side removed and a small amount of butter placed on it. Arrange on a baking tray and dust with crumbs. Grill for 3-4 minutes, or until crisp.

Smoked paprika prawn skewers

Prep:10 mins

Cook:10 mins

plus marinating

Serves 6 - 8

Ingredients

- ✓ 12 raw big prawns
- ✓ 1/2 tbsp smoked paprika (sweet or hot, whichever you prefer)
- ✓ Two finely chopped garlic
- ✓ 1 tsp cumin seeds, ground
- ✓ Two oregano sprigs, cut, or 12 tsp dried
- ✓ One large lemon, juice, and zest
- ✓ 2 tbsp olive
- ✓ You'll need:
- ✓ 12 miniature skewers

Method

1. Soak the skewers for 10 minutes in a dish of water. Meanwhile, peel and devein the prawns, leaving the tails intact. This is accomplished by

running a sharp knife down the back, producing a small incision large enough to remove the visible black vein. Prawns should be washed and patted dry with kitchen paper.

2. Combine the paprika, garlic, cumin, oregano, lemon zest, and 1 tbsp olive oil in a medium-sized bowl. Add the prawns and set them aside for 15 minutes at room temperature to marinate. After that, thread a prawn onto each stick.

3. Heat the remaining oil in a large frying pan and fry the prawns for 3-4 minutes, rotating halfway through or until just done. Batch processing may be required. Season with salt and pepper, sprinkle over little lemon juice and serve.

Spanish ham with crusty bread & chopped tomato

Prep:10 mins

Cook:5 mins

Serves 6

Ingredients

- ✓ 4 halved firm vine-ripened tomatoes
- ✓ 2 tbsp of your best olive oil
- ✓ 12 thick baguette slices
- ✓ One halved garlic clove
- ✓ Six serrano ham slices halved
- ✓ you will need
- ✓ 12 cocktails sticks

Method

1. On a dish, place a box grater and shred the tomatoes, leaving the skin behind. Drain the pulp through a small sieve, then season with 2 tbsp olive oil.

2. Brush with oil and toast or griddle the bread until golden. Rub one side with the garlic's sliced side. Spoon some tomato onto each slice just before serving. Finish with a piece of ham, a cocktail stick, and a sprinkling of freshly ground black pepper.

Printed in Great Britain
by Amazon

82465583R00059